Elena's Ride

by Susan Blackaby

Alone in the Arctic

by Diane Hoyt-Goldsmith

MODERN CURRICULUM PRESS

Pearson Learning Group

ISBN 1-4284-0400-7

Printed in the United States of America

2 3 4 5 6 7 8 9 10   10 09 08 07

1-800-321-3106
www.pearsonlearning.com

Contents

Elena's Ride

by Susan Blackaby

illustrated by Meryl Treatner

The sun was just edging over the tops of the trees as Elena made her bed. She straightened the pillows. She pulled the faded patchwork quilt into place, patting it smooth. Out her window, she could see her cousin and uncle. They walked across the courtyard, heading out toward the corral. Tío Diego, her uncle, waved his coffee mug in the air as he talked to Pepe. One of the dogs danced along between them. Already the sky was washed with a glimmer of clear, golden light.

Elena wondered what her mom was doing at that exact moment. Maybe she was still sleeping after a long night of studying. Maybe she was braiding her hair and planning her day. Maybe she had gotten up early too, and was packing her books and papers into Elena's old book bag. Maybe she was walking across campus to class.

Somewhere in the house, a clock chimed. It measured the hours in somber, even tones. Elena pulled her hair into a ponytail. Then she sat at her desk. She took out a piece of paper. She used colored pencils to make a sketch of the view from her window. Below it she wrote a note.

Dear Mama,

It is daybreak, and I am wide awake. I have been on the ranch only two weeks and already I can't sleep past 5:30. Pinch me! This can't be real! I miss you.

I love you,
E.

It had taken a few weeks for Elena to feel settled on her uncle's Texas ranch. For one thing, she missed her mom and dad. She had made a deal to stay for the summer. Her mom needed to go to school full time. Her dad was starting his new job as a pilot. But it wasn't easy to be away from them. For another, she was used to the color, variety, and noise of the city. Something new and unexpected was around every corner. On the ranch, there were no corners. The land stretched out to the horizon. It was broken only by the silver streak of the creek. To the west, the rugged mountains rose up sharply to meet the sky. The faint outline of the nearest town disappeared in the hazy glimmer of the highway. The city was a journey away.

On the ranch, one day seemed to fall into step behind the next. Elena worked with her cousin, Pepe. He patiently carried out repeated routines. Every job followed a set number of steps and movements. They were done in the same order and in the same way every time. Elena began to understand the slow, steady rhythm of saddling a horse, curling up rope, and unlatching and swinging open a gate.

Elena helped out with early morning chores. Once the animals were cared for and the rest of her jobs were finished, Elena was free to take her sketch pad and wander. She liked to go along the creek or up the canyons that led into the mountains. She always took one of the dogs with her, along with water and a snake-bite kit. She was learning about the earth and sky. Her parents, her grandparents, and even her great-grandparents had called this place home.

In the evenings, the family stayed at the dining room table long after the meal was cleared away. Pepe played with the wax that dripped down the big candles. The light flickered. Tío Diego told Elena stories about growing up on the ranch with her father and aunts.

Elena studied the portraits of her grandparents. The photos hung on the dining room wall. She had her grandmother's slim fingers and her grandfather's long, straight nose. Their dark eyes seemed to fill with laughter and life as Tío Diego talked about the family.

If only Elena could get used to the horses that Tío Diego raised. They were huge and powerful. Elena tried to be open-minded about learning to ride, but she was frightened. And she was sure the horses could sense it. Pepe teased her about being a chicken. She did not care. Riding made her stomach flip. Once she was up on the horse, the only thing that she could think about was how to get down. Tío Diego gave her jobs to do in the horse barn. They were supposed to help make her feel more at ease around horses, but they only magnified her fear. Tío Diego tried to find time for Elena to ride every day. She did not disobey his wishes, but she was happy when he was too busy to remember her lesson.

Elena sealed the envelope. Her bare feet slid over the cool, slick tile and slapped down the stairs to the main hall. In the kitchen, her Aunt Marta and Anna, the cook, greeted her.

"Ah, it is our sleepyhead," said Anna with a wink.

Tía Marta gave Elena a hug. "What is this?" Marta plucked the letter from Elena's hand. "Another letter!"

"Oh, I just write short letters," said Elena.

"Yes," said Anna. "Our Elena has only three things to say. I hate horses, I hate horses, and I hate horses. Is that right?"

Elena laughed. "I never said I hated horses! In fact, from far away, they are beautiful. Up close they are kind of big, but from far away, they are just right. I send Mama pictures too." Elena picked up a pen and made a quick sketch on a napkin. It showed a horse grazing by the creek. "See? Like that."

"That is a very tiny horse, Elena," said Tía Marta, looking closely at the drawing. "Hardly a steed! It's no bigger than a cricket. Nothing to be frightened of."

"Well, that's the way I like them," said Elena, accepting a mug of cocoa and a hot roll from Anna.

Tía Marta turned back to her work. "This land, these horses, they are in your blood, Elena. Sooner or later you will like to ride."

Elena gathered her supplies and went outside. A cool breeze stirred the shade under the porch. One of the dogs lifted its head as Elena passed by. It hopped up to follow. After a few steps it sat and waited, as if it needed permission to come along.

"Come along, Tip, unless you would rather stay here with these lazy old guys," said Elena.

Tío Diego waved as Elena and Tip passed by the corral. He was watching Pepe work with a colt. The colt was kicking up smoky puffs of dust.

Elena and Tip crossed the creek and a broad expanse of land before starting up a narrow trail. The trail followed a stand of pine trees that grew in a seam between the rocks. The rise was gentle. Elena could hardly tell that they were going up until she stopped to look back down the valley. The ranch buildings looked like little islands in a sandy sea.

The trail followed the tree line a little farther and then rose up, rocky and steep. Tip's feet skittered on the loose gravel. Elena was about to turn back when the trail suddenly leveled off onto a huge flat rock. Cliffs rose up on one side, and the valley stretched out below them.

Elena settled herself on a rocky ledge. She shared her water with Tip and then took out her sketch pad. She drew a picture of the rocky crags hanging in space. She wondered if her dad had climbed to this place and dreamed of becoming a pilot.

Dear Daddy,

I am up above the ranch, surrounded by sky. I hope it is cool and clear where you are too.

I miss you.

Love,

E.

Tip barked at the sound of crunching gravel. Elena looked up from her sketch pad to see Pepe on horseback, quickly side-stepping and skidding over the last part of the trail.

"Hey there!" said Pepe.

"Hi!" said Elena, jumping up. "How did you get up here?"

"Oh, it was a little bit tricky in places. But this steed is as sure-footed as a mountain goat."

Pepe leaned down and patted the horse's neck. "Good fella," he said quietly.

Tip's tail wagged. "Yeah, right. You too," laughed Pepe.

Elena looked at the horse's lathered neck and glistening body.

"I still can't believe you made it," she said.

Pepe hopped off his steed and took off the saddle bag. "Steady and fearless too. I am going to call him the Ridge Runner."

"Yeah, well you'd better park him away from the edge, or you can rename him Tumbleweed," said Elena.

"Good point!" said Pepe.

Pepe led the horse to a spot back against the cliff face. Then he pointed to a flat rock and motioned for Elena to join him.

"Anna packed us a picnic," he said. "I spotted you part way up the mountain and figured you might get hungry."

"You could see me from all the way down there?" Elena said.

"I saw your red shirt, silly," said Pepe, setting the food out on the rock. "You were pretty easy to spot until you got up into the trees."

"Well, it isn't as though I was hiding or running away or something."

"Oh, no," said Pepe. "You are only about fifty miles from the nearest riding lesson, that's all!"

"Hmm, well, I am starving," said Elena, reaching for a sandwich.

"Isn't this a cool place?" said Pepe. "If it were spring, a little creek would be running through here. We'd be sitting by a waterfall. I hardly ever come up here when it is dry like this."

Pepe shaded his eyes with his hand and looked up. His gaze rested on the cliff face. He pointed.

"Look up there," he said. "Do you think that is a cave?"

Elena could see a dark shadow in the rocks. It did look like an opening of some kind, but it was up too high to see clearly.

She shrugged. "I don't know. It could just be a nesting spot. Or it could lead to a lost mine."

"Do you think so?" said Pepe, looking surprised.

"Oh sure," said Elena. "Filled with silver and precious stones right up to the brim." She leaned back against a rock and started to make a sketch of Tip and Pepe.

"Well, I am going to investigate," said Pepe.

Before Elena had a chance to object, Pepe was scrambling up the rock face.

"Are you nuts?" she yelled. "What are you doing?"

"I'm just going to see what this is," Pepe called down to her.

"Come down! You're going to fall! Something terrible will happen! Don't do this!" Elena cried.

"I'm fine," called Pepe. "It's like climbing a ladder."

Pepe was lying flat against the rock face, gripping his fingers in a rock seam and feeling for a solid spot to put his foot. He moved like a spider, stretching and bending his way higher and higher. When he got up to the opening, he pulled himself up so that he was squatting, crouched on the narrow ledge.

"You were right!" he yelled. "It is a mine shaft! It looks pretty neat too!"

"Don't you dare go any farther, Pepe," yelled Elena.

"I won't," said Pepe, leaning into the shaft entrance. "I can't see much of anything anyway."

Just then there was a loud crack that echoed off the rock face. Elena was showered with tumbling pebbles. Pepe did not even have a chance to yell before the cave-in. He just disappeared into the darkness.

Elena screamed Pepe's name and then clapped
her hands over her mouth. She held her breath and
listened for Pepe's voice. Then she heard it, faint and
hollow, from deep inside the mountain.

"Elena! Elena! I'm OK! But get help!"

"Are you hurt?" she yelled, cupping her hands
around her mouth.

"No. But I'm stuck! Ropes! Bring ropes!"

Elena told Tip to stay put. Then she turned and ran to the horse. He nodded and stomped at the ground. She reached for the reins and threw them over his head. She quickly led him up beside a boulder so that she could boost herself up to mount. She got her foot in the stirrup and yanked on the pommel to pull herself up and swing into the saddle. Then, without hesitating for a moment, she took the reins and spun the horse around. She aimed for the place where the trail wound down through the rocks and ledges and trees.

The horse leaped forward. He plunged down the steep bank, sending rocks and gravel flying. Elena leaned into each turn, clinging to the horse's neck when he pitched forward, struggling to hang on as he slid. Once they were in the trees, Elena kept her head down. She ducked under low-hanging branches as the horse raced down through a blur of green. In one final leap, they reached the edge of the valley. Then Elena turned the horse toward the ranch.

"Hurry!" whispered Elena, and they flew at full gallop to get help.

Tío Diego had seen Elena coming down the mountain. He met her at the creek. She gasped for air as she told him what had happened.

"Tell Clara and Juan to meet me up on table rock," he said. Then he reached out and squeezed her shoulder.

"Go."

His eyes were somber, his voice was barely a whisper. His horse splashed across the creek and up the bank and Tío Diego was soon lost in a cloud of dust.

Elena rode on to the ranch and sent the two ranch hands back to help. Tía Marta made sure they took plenty of rope with them, and Anna gave them water and a first-aid kit. Then Elena and the women waited, keeping an eye on the tree line.

Elena walked the horse around the corral to cool him off. She inspected his legs to be sure that he had not hurt himself as he dove down the mountain. Then she brushed him and gave him food and water. She was just putting his tack away when she heard Tía Marta call. She hurried into the courtyard. Pepe was getting off Tío Diego's horse. Pepe was dirty and stiff. He gave Elena a sheepish grin. Tip ran up to her, wagging his tail.

"Were you scared?" Pepe asked.

"Yes! You fell head first into the mine! I'll say I was scared!" cried Elena. "I thought my heart was going to jump out of my mouth!"

Pepe had a confused look on his face. "No, not then. I mean when you were riding down the mountain on my horse. Were you scared?"

Everyone waited for Elena to answer.

A smile slowly lit up Elena's face. She had not been scared. During the ride she was fearless. Pepe's horse had carried her safely and swiftly down the mountain, as she knew he would.

"No, I wasn't," said Elena. "After all, horses are in my blood. And that horse is as sure-footed as a mountain goat. Which is more than I can say for some people!"

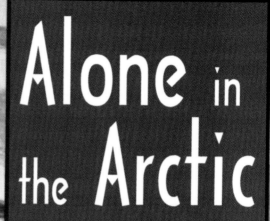

Alone in the Arctic

by Diane Hoyt-Goldsmith

illustrated by Jill Kastner

With each step, George's foot broke through a crust of ice. Sinking up to his knees in the snow, George made slow progress. It was bitterly cold, but his efforts brought beads of sweat to his forehead.

One more mile to go, George thought. He gazed into the distance. He could just see the coastline. The steel blue of the ocean separated one white world from another. Sky and land were the same cold color.

This was George's first trip into the wilderness alone. He had taken a packet of medicine a few miles up the river to one of the elders. Her name was Elly. She was so stiff with arthritis that she had trouble getting to town. She lived with her husband, Roy, and a few old sled dogs.

That morning, his father had said, "You are twelve now. I guess you can handle a job like this. Please walk over to Elly's, but wear my parka so you'll be warm enough. Just give her this medicine and come right back. We have only a few hours of light today."

Getting there had been easy. The day was nice enough and there were only a few miles to go. George had said hello to Elly and Roy. He petted the dogs and gave Elly her medicine.

Then a wind blew up from the west. Clouds began to form over the ocean. The sky got dark.

"You'd better start back now, young fella." Roy said with a smile. "Here. Take these crackers and some muktuk. You might need a snack on the way home."

George took the packet of crackers and pieces of raw whale blubber. He put them in the pocket of his dad's parka. "Thanks," he said.

George and his family lived near Nome, Alaska, on the edge of the Arctic wilderness. They were Inupiat (IN-yoo-payt), which in their language means "the people." For centuries, people like George and his family have survived in the far north by understanding the obstacles they faced.

With the coming of winter, George knew that a storm could mean danger. He was in a hurry to get home.

Leaving Elly's place, George decided to take a shortcut across Moonrise Creek. When he got there, though, the creek was deeper than he had ever seen it and twice as wide. It was a bigger obstacle than he had imagined. Still, George was determined to cross it.

He spotted a few old tent poles left over
from a fishing camp. He picked one up. It was
long enough.

Then he gazed at the creek. A few large slabs
of ice were floating downstream. "That's just
what I need," he said to himself. He leaned over
and jabbed the wooden pole into the ice. He
pulled it over to the bank. Then he stepped onto
it.

The piece of ice made a perfect raft. Slowly,
using all his strength, George poled his way
across the swollen creek. But it was tough going.
George fought the rushing current for each inch.

From the other bank of the creek, George had to climb up a steep hill. The wind came up suddenly. It blew snow into his eyes. Halfway up, George stepped on a slick rock. He slipped and fell, rolling all the way to the bottom of the hill.

Groaning, George checked himself carefully for injuries. His leg hurt so much he thought it might be sprained or broken. His cheek was sore. It bled a little where he had scraped it on the ice. And the storm was getting worse.

He'd lived all his life on the edge of the wilderness. George knew he had to do something fast. He wasn't far from home. But the storm was fierce. When weather overtakes an Arctic traveler, it can be dangerous. With his injuries, he knew it would be hard for him to walk. For a moment, his mind ran wild. He could only think the worst kinds of thoughts.

Then, suddenly, as if in a dream, George saw the face of his grandfather. He heard his grandfather's voice, soft and slow. He was telling stories about his childhood. He told about being lost in a storm. Grandfather told how he built up a pile of rocks. He stacked them one on top of another until they made a small tower. His family found the tower, and Grandfather too.

The memory gave George an idea. But first he had to do something about his leg. He took his jackknife out of his pocket. He cut into the white canvas parka cover. He tore off a strip of cloth. He wrapped it around his leg. It took a long time because George was in so much pain.

Meanwhile, it got colder and darker. The wind began to howl. Snow began to whirl. Soon the storm was roaring all around him. Ice crystals stuck to his face like shiny needles. George set to work. Hobbling on his hurt leg, he collected flat stones that were small enough to lift and carry. He brought ten or twelve to the top of an icy snow bank. He stacked them there until they took the shape of a person. There was even a little round stone for a head.

Then George took out his jackknife. He used it to carve out some ice from the crust that covered the snow bank. Then he dug into the snow like a dog. He scooped out a hole just big enough for his body. His grandfather said snow can keep you warm in a bad storm. It traps air as it falls. The air helps insulate you from the cold.

When the hole was large enough, George crawled inside and sat down. Once he was out of the wind, George was surprised that he didn't feel cold. His leg ached. "I can stand it," he said to himself. He had to.

Soon it was totally dark. The wind was howling and snow was piling up all around.

George felt his heart beating in his chest.
His thoughts were filled with confusion. This
happens sometimes when fear overtakes
a person. George began to feel frightened
and alone.

He put his hand into his pocket to get a
cracker. He felt something smooth.

He took it out of his pocket. It was a small
seal carved from a walrus tusk. His father
always carried it with him when he went
hunting. He told George that it brought
good luck.

The little seal was very old. George knew
that his grandfather had carved it one winter
long ago. He had heard the story of how
Grandfather had given the seal to his father
when he was a boy.

They had gone seal hunting that day.
George's father harpooned his first seal. George's
father had learned his lessons well. He had
crawled over the ice, trying to look and act like a
seal. When he was in range, he had thrown the
harpoon and hit the seal. Later, he gave the seal
meat to one of the elders in the village. On that
day, George's grandfather was very proud.

George was suddenly very tired. He closed
his eyes. His fist closed over the little seal and he
fell asleep.

The next thing he knew, his father and mother were shaking him.

"Wake up, George," they cried. "Are we ever glad to find you! We saw the rock pile you made, even in this awful storm. We knew you had to be close by."

The next time George woke up he was in his own bed. His body ached all over and he was thirsty.

"Have some water, son," his father said. He handed George a glass.

George noticed that the little seal was on the table next to his bed.

"Where did you find this?" he asked.

"You had it in your hand when we found you," his father answered. "I want you to have it. You proved to me that you are quite grown up now. Not everyone has the courage to take care of things the way you did. You made very sensible decisions out there!"

George looked over at the little seal and smiled.